Mary's Dust

Mary's Dust

- POEMS -

MELINDA MUELLER

with music by
LORI GOLDSTON

entre ríos books

ENTRE RÍOS BOOKS
www.entreriosbooks.com
Seattle, Washington

MARY'S DUST
Melinda Mueller, with music by Lori Goldston

ISBN: 978-0-9973957-4-7 (paper)

Cover image: *Reclining Dress Impression with Drapery*, life-size sculpture in cast glass ©2015 Karen LaMonte. Photo Credit: Martin Polak.

First Edition. ERB 006.
Printed in the United States by Edwards Brothers Malloy.

In honor of my line of Marys:

My great-grandmother, Margaret.
My grandmother, Marjorie.
My aunt, Marcia.

My mother, Maralyn.
She taught me to read
and gave me the world.

Contents

❧

Commit flight to memory,
for the bird is mortal.

— Forugh Farrokhzad
Delam Gerefteh Ast

ANNUNCIATION

The air before her congealed
and became the angel, blazing.

Its robes streamed and whirled
in a wind that filled her ears.

Through its transparent form
she could see the brown hills

and stunted trees beyond, magnified
and trembling like flames.

She could not have told
what was said. That story was

conceived years later, by men
who had not been there.

Afterwards the stirred dust
settled round her feet with a faint

ringing, as if it were the dust
of a thousand bells.

Maria Aegyptica

b. 344? – d. 421?

THE LOST GOSPEL OF MARIA AEGYPTICA

::1   *For true holiness is savage*, saith the Lord.
      It will rend you in its teeth for My sake.

1:17   I wished to go on the pilgrimage, but only
      that I might feed my body's desires in new pastures.

1:18   Therefore, I approached some comely-looking sailors
      and asked passage, saying, *I assure you, you will not*
      find me useless. And they laughed and took me.

1:28   I wandered the streets of Jerusalem
      hunting after the souls of young men,
      and willingly they fed themselves into my arms.

1:43   Yet each time I put my foot upon the church
      threshold, I was thrown back into the dust
      of the courtyard, until I was bruised with shame.

2:14   For seventeen years after I walked into this desert,
      lascivious songs prowled about my mind,
      and longing after wine, and meat, and men.

2:15   And then they all fell silent.

፠

3:9   I was beautiful. Now I am as you see me, sun-
blackened. Withered where once I was full
and soft. All the hair of my body matted
and gray as ashes, that once glowed like fire.

3:10   Naked and filthy, so that the stench
of my prayers may assault the heavens.

3:11   When I pray, my body rises from off the ground,
for it is a husk the wind might carry off.

3:12   When I step upon the Jordan, its ripples
are cobbles of stone, for I have become
a stick of dry wood, that water cannot slake.

፠

4:28   I beg you, come back this day a year from now, and pray
with me. It is above forty years since I have seen
either beast or man, or any shadow but my own.

4:29   Soon my shadow will desert me. Perhaps then
the Lord will relent, and have mercy on the nothing
I have made of myself, as an offering to Him.

Mariyah the Copt
b. ? [...] d. ?

MARIYAH THE COPT

In Medina when

[...] a Christian and a
concubine [...] scorned
though he is said [...]

[...] birth,
the last [...] all
his wives and [...]
named him Ibrahim

To [...] bitter
grief [...] infancy [...]
Of her [...] else
is [...]

[...] hyacinth is
how [...]

Marie Colinet, surgeon

b. 1560? – d. 1640?

WHAT SHE KNEW

♈

An art so steeped
In pain her patrons could not see
The beauty in it, though her work
Was much sought after.

♉

That her needlework, however
Fine, was stitched in mortal flesh.
It could not prevent the soul spilling
From its sack like grain.

♊

When she kept watch at a bedside
Through the night, she did not watch
Alone. She and that spectral
Sentinel were long acquainted.

♋

The body most often physicked
Itself, had its own midwifery
For birthing and dying, and she
Only handmaiden to that mistress.

♌

The compounding of poultices
To prevent corruption in a wound,
From wild pomegranate flowers,
Barley meal, and oil of roses.

♍

How to carve an infant,
Gasping Pygmalion, from its mother's
Womb and save them both. The which
She did accomplish forty times.

♎

What St. Thomas felt — as she puts her own
Hand into the gaping chest of a farmer
To wire his shattered ribs — was not doubt.
Rather, an almost insupportable

♏

Reprieve from grief.
That nothing she knew sufficed
To save her children when came
A visitation of the plague.

♐

The heart is a votive flame
Whose flickering she marks
In the wrists of the quick,
But is extinguished in the dead.

♑

How, when her husband — himself
A skillful surgeon — could not extract
A metal burr from the ironmonger's eye,
She might draw it out with a magnet.

♒

That the Earth must be an orb
Since the eye that sees it
Is, its garnet-flecked continent
Floating on a milky sea.

♓

In the briny depths beneath
The iris lay a soul's mysteries,
Its lost maps, mirrors,
Monsters. And the drowned.

THE REPENTANT MAGDALEN

Oil on canvas, Georges de La Tour, circa 1640

How have we not seen it, what she did,
What she and the other women
Must have done? They are gathered
On that Sabbath night, still flayed with grief
And horror — though not, it must be said,
With fear, knowing themselves safe in their
Insignificance. Whereas the men, elsewhere,
Hiding, have ample cause to be afraid. The men

Would slip back to their boats, wouldn't they?
They would wave off questions, they would
Deny. They would name it mirage, or the patriot
Despair of a people occupied; the same goad
Drives — they plead for understanding — insurgents
In the hills, the Zealots? Call it a fruitless
Dream. The women remember every

Word of it, that dream. It would follow
The Baptist into murdered silence. Say
It is Martha, then, head gripped in her
Wretched hands, who cries out, "It would
Need a miracle ..."

They left the shroud with its brutal stains
Tossed down, as a man might fling aside
His bedclothes. At dawn, the Magdalene
Went and told them that had been with Him
As they mourned and wept ...

Then arose Peter, and ran unto the sepulcher;
And stooping down, he beheld the linen cloths
Laid by themselves …

The men drank that hope, they became
Apostles, they went to their several
Martyrdoms rejoicing.

There was a certain other tomb
The two sisters could attend — would be
Expected to attend. At some later time
The rattling bundle was taken up once more;
The relics scattered against discovery;
Lazarus left alone with his second death.

Her fingertips rest — and with such tenderness —
On a skull historians call Allegory for the wages
Sin demands. No matter whether
Sleepless, late, lost in the candle's writhing
Light, she calls it by another, secret
Name. Nor does she repent.

Mary Frith

b. 1584? – d. 26 July 1659

MOLL CUTPURSE SINGS THE BLUES

"Enter Moll in a frieze jerkin and a black safeguard."

Bing close, my darling partridges,
    Bing close as all you can,
Look close as you may please, partridges —
    See you a woman or a man?

While you ponder if I'm feathered
    As a swan or swain
Watch your pockets aren't unfeathered
    By my crew plucking game.

    I'll play my worst for you,
    Cut your purse for you.
    I'm a roarer, and a cloyer —
    So say you, say you, say you.

You cheer your pretty lads on stage
    Lassie-rigged inside a dress.
I strut in breeches on your stage,
    You shout me scandalous.

Man or woman, long or deep,
    No matter I'm yclept —
Thus may a woman earn her keep
    Yet not be stallion-kept.

> *I'll play my worst for you,*
> *Cut your purse for you.*
> *I'm a roarer, and a cloyer —*
> *So say you, say you, say you.*

You hear my lute, I play my heart,
    Care's rack has tuned its strings.
You taste the sweet of your sweetheart,
    I bear love's bitter stings.

Whether all the hours of lightmans
    Cast I one shadow or a pair,
Once come the hours of darkmans
    All go in shadows there.

> *I'll play my worst for you,*
> *Cut your purse for you.*
> *I'm a roarer, and a cloyer —*
> *So say you, say you, say you.*

MARY EASTY

Thus is she ferried
over the River Jordan at last
in the mouths of ants,
for her bones are flaking.

For the hide beetles have unstrung
her thews and sinews.

For her flesh has been rendered
to grave wax by the acids of her own decay,
and cheese moths and scuttle flies
dabble their tongues in her drippings.

For she is become gravid
with maggots, whose churning
rocks her corpse from side to side.

For her specter appears again
to Mary Herrick, crying,
Vengeance! Vengeance!

For her skin blisters and slips from her limbs.

For fluid seeps from her mouth and her eyes.

For her eyes and her tongue protrude,
and her torso bloats and splits open
from death's exhalations.

For her skin marbles black and green
as bacilli swarm along her veins.

For the lining of her veins congeals
and the trapped blood darkens to purple.

For a paste of flies' eggs coats her mouth
and lies beneath her eyelids,

for the flesh flies have found her in minutes;
they will attend upon her,
being faithful unto death.

For she is flung with the others
into crevices among the rocks.

For eight "firebrands of hell" hang from the tree.

For her lungs are two wasps' nests;
their fiery wasps boil in her chest.

For she chokes in the noose.

For through the muslin hood
the world is a patchwork of shadows
and brightness.

For she has tendered her family
her farewells, and prayed with them.

For though the cart cried out and balked
under its load, they are brought to the hilltop.

For from her gaol cell her specter
appears to Mary Herrick, saying,

On the morrow
I go upon the ladder to be hanged
for a witch. But I am innocent.

Maria Sibylla Merian

b. 2 April 1647 – d. 13 January 1717

MARIA SIBYLLA MERIAN

"The crocodile is certainly a fierce insect,"
and cabbages' many-folded wombs give rise
to worms? The whole matter is in disarray.
Does belief in God permit spontaneous generation,
or (*Aquinas*) are maggots born of meat the Devil's work?
The wealthy cram their cabinets with curiosities

lacking system. She knows better. Her curiosity
since girlhood has fixed itself upon insects.
She has opened the pupa's clockwork
case, from which the silk-moth will rise
to daub its blown-glass eggs, which generate
the larvae in their turn; these then array

themselves in silken cloaks — and fall to disarray,
to soup — the caterpillar unmade. "That Curious
Person Madame Maria Merian," third-generation
engraver (though a woman), draws her insects
in time-lapse, from egg to butterfly, having raised
them in boxes full of leaves. Her work

is thus a philosophy, a new theory on the Works
of God — though fecund Surinam very nearly disarrays
both her studies and her health. She rises

before the sun's blast, and importunes the curious
locals (an unescorted white woman, seeking insects!)
for information: Which larva generates

which butterfly? It will, in fact, be generations
before the answers are known. The butterflies work
in color guilds, according to the light or shade. Insects
of one species vary by juvenile diet, arrayed
to mimic their food, which they "see," curiously,
with their bellies. Six fresh mysteries arise

for each accomplished fact, like new heads rising
when you slice a dragon's neck. To generate
certainty is easier in chilly climates. Her curios
are packed, at length; she sets sail to finish the work
at home, in Amsterdam. In Europe's gray light, she arrays
her discoveries in tropic carmine red, an insect-

generated pigment in whose use she excels. Her insects
rise lively from the page and from the plants they feed on; arrayed
in knowledge, a metamorphosis of curiosity into learnéd work.

Mary Wortley Montagu

26 May 1689 (baptized) – d. 21 August 1762

MARY WORTLEY MONTAGU in CONSTANTINOPLE

Lady Mary breakfasts on the pomegranate's boon, a rubied heart,
and sweet. Lifting gouts of seeds with a silver spoon, she empties that heart.

❧

At the *hammam*, Sophia's women uncloak their nakedness like lamps.
England's pox-plagued. Lady Mary is a scarred moon, beauty's ruined heart.

❧

Lady Mary eloped for passion but found none. Here women venture
to their lovers, concealed in veils from the gilded noon. It stings her heart.

❧

Of stays beneath her skirts, "They think my husband locked me in that machine."
Like windswept candle flames, the dancers swoon, rousing Lady Mary's heart.

❧

Lady Mary sits at her window, watching dusk's shawl drift down. In lore
the nightingale, forlorn for the rose, croons to its many-chambered heart.

❧

The Sultan's so mad for tulips that at night, tortoises with lanterns
on their backs light his gardens; restless moons, like the lantern of her heart.

Lady Mary visits a Sultan's widow, self-exiled into mourning;
an isle Mary sailed to by another course, marooned in her own heart.

From her inkwell she draws forth a world unknowable to men: At the baths,
a bride in naught but plaited hair. Silk cocoon of the *harem*'s heart.

The ambassador's recalled. From *jasmina*-scented stars and honeyed sun,
Lady Mary goes home to grey. Each month a scimitar moon pricks her heart.

Maria Gaetana Agnesi
b. 16 May 1718 – d. 9 January 1799

THE WITCH

$$y = a^3/(x^2 + a^2)$$

Let there be a circle of radius **a** with center at {0, **a**}.

Let there be a horizontal line **L** passing through {0, **2a**}.

Draw a line passing through the Origin
　　　and any point **M** on the circle.

Let the intersection of this secant and line **L** be **N**.

The resulting curve is the locus of intersections
　　　of a vertical line passing through **N**
　　　and a horizontal line passing through **M**.

Let this curve be called the *Curve of Agnesi,*
　　　for the woman of Milan
　　　who worked out its equation.

Let us then confuse *aversiera* (a curve,
　　　derived from the Italian term
　　　for the rope that turns a sail)
with *avversaria* (the adversary,
　　　which is to say, the Devil,
　　　but here of feminine gender
　　　and thus the Devil's consort).

The resulting translation is the *Witch of Agnesi,*
    and by this name her solved curve is still known.

Let our mind's eye be drawn with hers
    from the manuscript on which she labors,
    out her father's windows. Vineyard trellises
    in parallel curves describe the camber of the hills,
above which the sun explicates its quotidian arc.

From the intersection of these sets of curves the seasons are derived:
    when to prune the vines;
    when to burn those that are diseased;
    when to harvest the grapes.

In her time the seasons of Black Death are subsided,
    and the Great Hunger,
    the Western Schism, the Inquisition,
    Malleus Maleficarum,
    St. Anthony's Fire:
All those lines of history from the loci of whose intersections
    derived the hunt for witches, and their burning.

Therefore: Let her die in an austerity of her choosing,
    Blue Nun of the Hospice Trivulzio,
and despite the proposition's converse:
    That Europe's last convicted witches
    will burn in Poland two years hence.

Anna Maria dal Violin

b. 1696 – d. 1782

CONCERTO FOR ANNA MARIA DAL VIOLIN

The body of a violin is mostly air.

Venezia, a city built of water.

With my bow and the Maestro's music
I shall set that air on fire.

Though you drained Venezia dry
You could not quench that sound.

We foundling girls, we are like our violins —
Of substance, very little.

In our near nothingness the music resonates,

As in the church bells' open throats,
In the hollow bones of organ pipes,

In the utter emptiness of angels.

They are music, I think —
The angels. Music unfettered
From all earthly instruments.

When I play, I feel their feathers
All about me in the air.

Marie Antoinette

b. 2 November 1755 – d. 16 October 1793

prisoner number 280

16 OCTOBER 1793

Being bereft of everything, she kneels
by the cold cot and prays the rosary
of her bereavement —

of the King;
and of her husband, the King;
and of her lover not her husband;

of the dauphin dead of his deformities;
of his brother kidnapped for *liberté*;
of a daughter dead an infant;
and of the daughter who will survive her;

of her moonlight skin and the dense gold tumble
    of her hair;
of gowns like reefs of jewels;
of candelabras, carriages,
    horses and the scent of oiled leather;
of feasts both holy and profane;

of her frivolity;
of feathery hats
   à la circonstance,
   à l'Iphigenie,
   à l'inoculation,
   à la mode of the fickle weather
of public enthusiasms;
of orange-water and ether
   for her fainting spells;

of the Princesse de Lamballe, superintendent
   of the Queen's household;
of the chief lady-in-waiting;
   the bedchamber women,
   the Body Apothecary,
   the Reader to the Queen,
   the clerks of the linen cupboard;

of her German tongue;
of the world into which she was born
   and for which she was tutored;
of *long live the queen.*

She kneels next
for the guillotine's benediction.

Mary Wollstonecraft

b. 27 April 1759 – d. 10 September 1797

CHILDBED FEVER

    1.   *William Godwin, her widower.* April 1798.

The rambunctious bulbs muscle up
out of the dirt — they are, aren't they,
a little ghoulish. They roll their stone aside
and stand erect for Judgment Day.
And Creation seems so cheerful
on the subject: All that trash of apple blossoms
tumbled on the ground, pink and white.
As if it were nothing, what wind does
to the trees: first the flowers and later
the leaves flayed off the branches.

    2.   *Mary Shelley, her daughter.* April 1816.

Well, there is no sorrow in these lads
of spring, the green sprouts or tatters
of snow. The snow melts without regret,
of course. So do nearly all the living
wither, fade or batter themselves to death
on window-panes, ignorant of grief.
The weather warms. A fly leaves
her thousand offspring crawling in decay
to live or die as may be. No grief there.
But we cannot regard the world without
making it a mirror. Glistening mushrooms

rise dispassionate from summer's ruins,
out of beauty corrupted into oozing crumbs,
and we assign to them our horror.

    3.   *Her Ghost.* April.

Grief emerges out of warm blood's meager
issue. We hover in fur or feathers over our tiny
handful, our hearts one stopped heartbeat
from hopeless loss. The floor of the world
is a thinly frozen lake, and we must cross it
with our children in our arms. From the shore
we'll never get to, last year's dead ranks
of rush-grasses wave to and fro
in unison: *Come on. Come on.*

Mary Darby Robinson

b. 27 November 1757? – d. 26 December 1800

SHE GOES UPON THE STAGE AS ROSALIND

> *… a wandering beauty is a blade out of its scabbard.*
> *You know how dangerous …*
> —John Crowe Ransom, *Judith of Bethulia*

Enter Rosalind, with her legs unsheathed
Of their skirts. Every blade in the theatre
Stands *en garde* before "Ganymede" has breathed
A line. Such dangerous games are sweeter

The more dangerous. Does wearing breeches
Breach the gates of her virtue? The question
Profits the house. The Crown Prince beseeches
Her, with ardent letters, to indiscretion —

Which is his aphrodisiac. For love,
It seems, he will risk all. *Ah, men have died
And worms have eaten them, but not for love.*
He leaves her undone and penniless beside.

Beauty, though a weapon wielded by who wears it,
Proves a guardless sword that wounds her when she bares it.

Mary Prince
b. ? – d. after 1833

SALT, A SLAVE NARRATIVE

salt is the sea's ghost	sun eats water's flesh
immortal salt remains	a dazzle in the salt ponds

> *At night, hot light-bursts trouble the slaves' closed eyes,*
> *From the day's sun-blaze, sea-blaze, blaze of salt-crystals.*

puddle clay into empty ponds	the sky is a kiln
for firing the clay	and I a pot in its furnace

> *At night, the slaves are portioned a meal of black bread,*
> *And brackish water — If it's Sunday, a scrap of salt-cod.*

the windmills screech	with flailing arms
they drag the sea onto land	to be burned

> *At night, there are salt-bags to wash out, salt to be raked clean,*
> *Salt to shovel into the bags, bags to be hauled to the docks …*

wade in the sea-bittern	scoop salt slurry into heaps
to drain Lot's-wives	ghost-stones over graves

> *At night, the slaves sleep on planks, in stalls. They lay down*
> *Hanks of grass to ease their legs, whose salt-boils never heal.*

the wind's too weary to blow	windmills standing idle
I'm to turn the pump	for they cannot flog the wind

At night, salt crystals form in the sky. The Milky Way
Is a slurry, seeping bitter mother liquor onto the Earth.

lips salty   arms salty   breasts dripping brine
my soul is salt   trying to flee from my body

      for the soul is a free thing   *it hates its fetters*

Mary Anning

b. 21 May 1799 – d. 9 March 1847

STRATIGRAPHY

Sunset bleeds marrow in the bone-grey sky —
The wind is up. Storm-waves, my unpaid quarrymen,
Are sledging *ammonoids* from the cliffs below Black Ven.
Someone else must sort the rubble, for shortly I
Must yield my own bones to the clay, and pray the Lord
Unearth them at the Judgment. Will He raise
All His creatures, think you, at the End of Days —
Will my fiendish *pterodactyl* soar again, as it soared
In its own epoch? If I seem chimerical, it is the laudanum
Makes me so — Oh, but Cuvier thought my *plesiosaurus*
A counterfeit chimera, "a serpent pulled through a tortoise,"
Until my proofs robbed his sting of all its venom.
I did so enjoy an opposition amongst the bigwigs.
There came a time they all knew who I was —
The first to pry an *ichthyosaur* from the Blue Lias,
And I but twelve. I used to set my dog to guard my digs,
Until a landslip killed him, and I just spared —
And at my feet, *megalosaurus*. Folks say fire's luck
Led me to my "stone dragons," for lightning struck
When I was a babe, and left three beside me dead.
It was fire that named me, for my parents had a Mary
Before me, that died in a house fire, and I was christened
In her memory. My *belemnosepia*'s fossil ink glistened
Black in Philpot's drawing of it, after all those ages buried,
And I thought: What might not be saved? Even my lost sister
Mary, and *Mary* my mother, and *Mary* myself. Let Heaven sort
Our bones — Or perhaps I shall assist, since I know the work.
Say my work is my fruitful issue, though I die a spinster.

Mary Ann Lamb

b. 3 December 1764 – d. 20 May 1847

CONSIDER THE ODD MORPHOLOGY OF REGRET

And how it changes. It teeters, a great insect,
across the floor on legs too thin, too
long, too many to keep track of, and yet
how quickly it's upon you, its membranous

wings whirring on your upraised arms. Next
it's squirming puppies in your dream, tied
inside a sack for drowning, while you beg
please don't, please don't, and your beloved

shrugs and cinches the knot. It is an egret,
icy white and motionless, and you the ditch
it fishes in, you the thrashing frog it gets
clamped in its beak. The deformed child flaps

its awful arms to be picked up but you let
it howl for comfort. If you could take it to you,
if you could not avert your eyes when it set
its lumpen head against your breast …

It cries, it drools, it lifts its stumps and pets
your neck. It shifts into a thing with claws
and lipless teeth, then a writhing grub, eggs
spilling from its gut. If you held it long

enough, no matter what it did, would the debt
at last be paid; would you find it is
yourself asleep in your own arms, every defect
soothed? Would you be permitted to forget?

COVERT ACTS

PVT. M. GALLOWAY. *Field hospital near Antietam.*
September 18th, 1862.

I am discovered. After months of going off alone to piss
in the woods — as they all do, anyway, the latrines being so foul —
and to bleed there, monthly, but then, we all bled, didn't we,
one way or another?

After sleeping clothed, and bathing clothed, and that, too,
no different from the rest, all of us clothed in grime
no laundry is the equal to, unless the angels'
washing-house in heaven,

after pitching my voice low enough to pass,
after smudging my chin with coffee grounds
and acting stubble-proud like all the boys,

after learning to smoke, and learning to swagger, and swear,
and fire a rifle under fire, and to stomach hardtack and maggot-ridden
bacon,

after answering to reveille, advance, retreat, hold-the-line,
hold-your-fire and fire-at-will,

after "fix bayonets!" and "damn your eyes!"

After all that some Rebel boy, *damn his eyes*, puts a ball
in my chest, and there's no hiding what else is there

when Miss Barton — thank God it was a woman, anyway —
peels the filthy woolens from the wound. And looks me
in the eyes, and almost smiles.

M. E. WALKER. Field Surgeon. *Battle of Chickamauga.*
September 18th – 20th, 1863

Walking among the stretchers, I imagine them, these boys
and men, running in the battlefield — the battle-*woods* —
through slabs of light, and falling under the weight of it.

And as each falls, his foolish heart keeps closing on fistfuls
of blood, until it has wrung the body dry. Or if not, if
they make it this far, gangrene likely does the job instead.

First they look at you, eyes mad with terror, and then
they start to sink away, back and down a fathomless
well of thought, farther and farther, and out of sight.

And out of sight. And if the last face they saw
was a woman's, mine, a woman dressed in trousers
so I could stand in their blood not in a skirt sopping

with the weight of it, does anyone suppose it can
have mattered? Or that my own heart will not,
from the sight of all this dying, also wring me dry?

M. E. Bowser, aka "Ellen Bond." Union Spy.
Home of Jefferson Davis, Richmond. 1864.

Slow-

witted.   Un-

lettered.   Of no

account

on account

of my black skin.

They have no idea. They talk among themselves as if I were deaf.
They leave their papers lying on their desks. The which I read

while dusting, and remember perfectly. Eidetically. From the Greek,
εἶδος, meaning "to see." I see and am unseen. Their blindness will be

their undoing. *As it is for all my nighted children,*
my Lord, my *only* Lord, reminds me

when I pray for my salvation and deliverance
from evil. And that He will keep me hidden from their sight.

Marie Laveau

b. 10 September 1801 – d. 15 June 1881

ST. LOUIS CEMETERY NO. 1

It's the living haunts the dead.
Their pleadings worry up a turbulence
round my tomb.   *make him love me   bring*
me wealth   cure my sickness   visit
trouble on my enemy   make us
wealthy   fix my troubles
give me a child   oh mamma marie
bring me   love me   give me
cure me

Been nothing of the yellow-jack
a long time now, but rumors
of another plague that's shifting
the quick to the dead.

The dead don't trouble me, no.
They brought my daughter here,
and her bones fell out
from her flesh into dust
of my arms. There's no lonely
in amongst the dead.

The dead's all old, and settled,
even the infants. The living
is all children, scratching Xs

on my wall, scraping up goofer dust
to make their gris-gris, leaving
trinkets for me — as if
I were a *lwa* or a saint.

They paint their window shutters
blue, and blue all round their porches,
to keep bad spirits out. Children,
all the sky's haint blue, and still
your troubles find you.
Nothing I can do for that. The dead is as helpless
as the living. It just don't scare us anymore.

Mary Kelly

b. 1863? – d. 9 November 1888

MARY KELLY

She importunes a customer on Thrawl Street,
her skirt draggling in the alley's refuse,
red shawl tugged round her shoulders ...

> Five in the literature are called
> canonical, meaning it is certain
> their provenance is his. The first
>
> of these was Mary Ann (called
> "Polly") Nichols. The last was
> Mary Kelly. At the inquest,
>
> witnesses say she was a quiet woman,
> when sober. That night, she was not
> sober. Witnesses say she woke them
>
> singing, "A Violet from My Mother's
> Grave." Witnesses say she once
> lived in France; that she called herself
>
> *Marie Jeanette* thereafter. That she
> was Irish. That she earned her doss
> in the usual way for a woman of her

circumstances. Witnesses say she was
"fair pretty." In the one photograph,
collops of her flesh lie on the bedside table.

... red shawl tugged round her shoulders,
for the night is raw. A witness says she put
her hand on the man's chest, laughing, *All right,*
my dear, come along. You shall be comfortable.

Mary Henrietta Kingsley

b. 13 October 1862 – d. 3 June 1900

POSTHUMOUS LETTERS
OF MARY HENRIETTA KINGSLEY

"I am no more human than a gale of wind is."

First, the white crown and broad, blue
shoulders of Mt. Tenerife materialized
upon the just-paler blue of the sky, as if
from that sky the mountain was a crystalline
precipitate. And later, after passing through the forge
of an equatorial sunset, the sky cooled to black
drizzled thick with stars, mirrored in a starry sea.
Thus was I exposed to Africa, an affliction
from which I have desired no cure.

Love? I answer as did Laplace,
when Napoleon inquired why
God did not figure in his discourse
on Saturn's orbit: *I have no need*
of that hypothesis. Well, but I commit
a pomposity. I ought in truth to say
that love has had no need of me.

Lest you be tempted to pity: When tropic flocks of birds
come to roost at day's end, they first fly to and fro
above the trees, each bearing its skein of air,
and when at last they subside among the leaves,
a great soft fabric settles down over everything.

There is no lover like a loved place; no one
so various or constant as my rivers murmuring
their lissome thoughts all through the night.
I wished neither other shelter nor other comfort.

The Calabar believe each person
possessed of four souls:
a creature of the forest
that is your bush soul;
another soul that casts your shadow;
a dream soul whose wanderings
you see while sleeping;
and the eternal soul.

This last soul is merely loaned to you;
it will never forsake this earth
as you do, when you die. *Come back,
come back, this is your home,*
friends cry out to one dying.
Only the fourth soul will answer —
through newborn eyes.

I met my bush soul, one night on a lake
of the Kâkola River. From the forest
emerged a luminous violet ball,
which flitted along the pale sand selvage
of the far shore. I paddled across
to collect this curious specimen.
When I drew near, it plunged
into the water, glowing as it sank,
until it vanished in the depths. There
was my future leave-taking foretold —
a sea-change that caused me no surprise

and but little regret. Oh my friends:
Forgive me. I loved you as much
as I was able, with my peg-leg of a heart.

Mary Fields

b. 1832? – d. 1914

STAGECOACH MARY

One of the freest souls ever to draw a breath — or a thirty-eight.
~Gary Cooper

The wind was a wolf; The wolves were a gale;
The snow was as cold as the stars;
The night sank down into its black hours,
When Mary carried the mail.

Her four horses foundered; A wheel axle failed;
The wagon-bed yawed on the ice.
The ravening wolfpack closed in like a vise
On Mary who carried the mail.

"Do you think I'm a-frighted? Do you think I'll turn tail?"
She chambered a round and took aim.
"I've faced worse than this in a hot poker game.
Black Mary won't scare from this mail."

"Let the cold grind its teeth; Let the winter wind wail;
Let hell's hounds stalk me in shifts.
I'm as mean as this storm, as tall as these drifts.
Black Mary will carry the mail."

She stood like a mast; Her greatcoat was a sail
On a pirate ship rigged for a battle.
She lit her cigar; She uncorked her bottle,
And planted one foot on the mail.

"Since you're all gathered round, I'll tell you a tale,"
She called to the wolves that besieged her.
"How this black woman done whatever it pleased her;
And why Mary carries the mail."

"I met up with some nuns, and I followed their trail,
Till the bishop dismissed me for fightin'.
But the Mother Superior, she put a word right in,
To pay me to carry this mail."

She spun out her stories, till at last the sky paled,
And the wolfpack surrendered its vigil.
She unhitched her team, she shouldered her satchel,
And Mary carried the mail.

TESTIMONY

I.   11 DECEMBER 1911

Mary Bucelli, called as a witness on behalf of the People,
being first duly sworn, testifies as follows:

    Q. How long were you employed by the Triangle Shirtwaist
       Company?

    A. Two years — nearly two years.

    Q. And were you in their employ and in their factory
       on the ninth floor on March 25, 1911?

    A. Yes.

    Q. Every night when you ceased to work and went out
       was there a watchman standing there?

(Objected to as leading. Sustained.)

    Q. Was there anyone standing there?

    A. Yes. He would examine the pocketbook.

    Q. And was there any other way to get out
       excepting that passageway?

*(Objected to as calling for a conclusion of the witness,
and as incompetent. Sustained.)*

    Q. You spoke of someone looking at your pocketbook.

    A. It was compulsory. He wouldn't let us pass
       unless we did so.

Q. You opened it and showed him you were not taking
any goods or embroidery or lace.

A. Yes.

Q. When you were at work, where did you sit?

A. The last time, you mean?

Q. Yes.

A. Fourth row, near the window.

Q. And how did you know there was a fire?

A. I didn't see any fire, but I saw the girls at the door,
and they were shouting and screaming.

Q. When you got to the door, what did you do?

A. I tried to open it, but I couldn't.

*(Objected to as calling for a conclusion of the witness,
and as incompetent. Sustained.)*

Q. What did you do to try to open it?

A. I took hold of the handle and I turned it
and I pulled it towards me.

Q. Did the door open?

A. No.

Q. After you failed to get out of that door
where did you go?

A. I followed the other girls, and when I saw them all
going in one direction I said to myself,
If we all go that way we will get killed, and I
broke a window, and went on the fire escape.

Q. Did you have to get onto the table to get to the fire escape?

(Objected to as incompetent. Objection sustained.)

Q. What did you jump on to, to get to that fire escape?

A. The tables that the shirtwaists were on.

Q. How did you get down?

A. The fire escape.

Q. Have you now any doubt in your own mind
   about the movements that you have testified to here today?

*(Objected to as asking a witness
to corroborate herself. Sustained.)*

II.   25 MARCH 1911

Now another of the girls has climbed out
Onto a ninth floor windowsill, having
Found no other exit. She opens

Her pocketbook, and pours its contents
Over those gathered below. She has not taken
Any goods, or embroidery, or lace.

She lifts off her hat (which she had trimmed
Herself, quite smartly), sweeps out
Her arm, and sails the hat as she might

Have tossed a bouquet at her wedding,
Since she will never marry, now. The hat
Twirls through smoke and gently down.

Finally, and in spite of the objections
Screamed by the crowd — for these are overruled
By flames clawing out the window

At her back — having corroborated herself
As best she can, before witnesses,
She steps forward, into the incompetent air.

GHOST BIRDS:
1920 Federal Census, Island of Moloka'i, Leper Settlement

'Ula-'ai-hāwane.   A small bird
patterned in black, gray, and red.
Last seen in the early 1890s in Kohala.
Habits and voice unknown.

Mary Kaihi.   Inmate.
Bishop Home for Unprotected Leper
Girls and Women.   Age 14.   Single.
Has attended school.   Can read.   Can write.
Trade none.

Oahu oo.   Has not been seen
since 1837.   Inmate.
McVeigh Home for Caucasian Patients.

Mary Smith.   Probably conspicuous
in flight.   Nothing else is known.

Mary Kawaipola.   Inmate.
Kalaupapa Hospital.   Age 19.
Voice: usually silent.   Early accounts describe
a clear but quiet whistled song. Single.
Has attended school.   Can read.   Can write.

Miriam Kahua.   Has not
been reported since the 1860s.

Hawaiʻi oo.   Immature entirely black.   Inmate.
Kalaupapa Nursery.   Age 2 months.
Little else is known about it.

Mary R. E. Leimape.   Presumed
extinct.   Voice a long,
plaintive whistle.

Kioea.   Widowed.   Last seen
in 1859 near Kaumana.   Inmate.
Bayview Home for Aged and Helpless.

Mary Ward.   Kalaupapa Hospital.   Age 19.
Trade none.   Curious — would approach an observer.
Has attended school.   Can read.
Can write.   Known only
from Molokaʻi.   Last seen in 1907.

Mary Lavelave.   Last seen early in 20th century,
and probably extinct.   Age 15.   Single.
Can read.   A loud melodious voice.

Mary Ann Ah Kiona.   Survived
into 1960s in Alakaʻi Swamp.
Possibly now extinct everywhere.

Akialoa.   An introduced population
destroyed by rats during World War II.

Mary Kaiheluolii.   Last seen
on Moloka'i, 1904.   Inmate.   Bishop Home
for Unprotected Leper Girls and Women.
Voice a loud *oh oh*.

Oloma'o.   Endemic to Hawai'ian islands
of Lānai (last seen 1933), Maui (extirpated
by historic times), and Moloka'i,
where it clings precariously to existence.
Frequently calls from concealment.

Inmate.   Has attended school.   Can read.
Can write.   Trade none.   Possibly extinct,
but rumors of its existence persist.   Is said
to have escaped extinction by feeding on seabird eggs
when rabbits destroyed all vegetation.

Song is a long, thrush-like, somewhat
halting melody, with a ventriloquial quality.
Now seldom (if ever) sings.

Mary Cassatt

b. 22 May 1844 – d. 14 June 1926

MARY CASSATT, AFTER 1915

Blind now, and bereft of any art for what she sees. For blindness is not, as is commonly supposed, a moonless night, simple dark in place of sight. She wishes it were so. There is a relentless canvas — no, a copper plate, incising itself upon her retinas; she cannot discern objects *as* objects separate from her eyes. What she noticed first was everything crowded forward onto a single plane, which was ironic, since that was what she had learned to do: flatten her subjects onto the canvas, yet have them seem to float free of it. Things stopped floating freely *en plein air*: She could no longer distinguish far from near. She might, perhaps, have painted *that*, except she had begun to fumble for her brushes, nor could she modulate her brushstrokes — though for a time she tried to recognize by *smell* the pigments on her palette. Monet, she knows, was able to make an art of *going* blind. Not, however, of blindness itself, another sense entirely. Phosphenes shower through her vision like meteors; colors slide off their objects, as when wind muddles a reflection in water. Everything is smears on her eyes, and will not resolve. Brilliant sunlight registers, but only as a heightening of the chaos. Night is calmer, is mostly just the phosphenes. She has begun to see sounds, or perhaps merely to assign them to what has become otherwise inscrutable: a growing scarlet intrusion from her left (A-major), or the intermittent cerulean flashes (D-minor, struck *sforzando*). It strikes her now that she had filled her works with mirrors, as if she knew she must double all she saw, before she was forsaken of all seeing ...

Maria Salomea Skłodowska

b. 7 November 1867 – d. 4 July 1934

RADIUM

As, in her native Poland, the ember-colored
fox ignites the stubble field it streaks across,
ignites even the noonday dusk of the forest floor.

As, toddling into her parents' long-ago garden
after dark, and crouching beside a lantern there,
she cried out: *Look. The ants. They have shadows.*

As religionists rummaged in the body for its soul,
that ant-shadow, which might "be shown on an X-ray
plate as a lighter spot on the dark shadow of the bone."

So she fractionates the soul of pitchblende,
and having pent it in a glass vial, gazes into
its blue dazzle. And it gazes into her, being

the abyss Nietzsche warned of. And ransacks her.
And ignites her bones to ash. *Heaven doth with us as we
with torches do.* Nor will she lift from it her hands.

Mary Mallon
b. 23 September 1869 – d. 11 November 1938

MARY MALLON

[The lights come up. A woman stands stage left.
She wears an apron; across one cheekbone is a cicatrix
of flour. She is kneading dough on a table before her.]

[A man in a severe suit enters from behind her,
stage right. He appears to expostulate, referring
to a notebook in one hand.]

[The woman rounds on him, raising
a kitchen knife. He retreats offstage.
The lights go down.]

[Children's chorus]
> *Mary, Mary, what do you carry?*
> *One, a pudding, two, a cake,*
> *Three, a case of dysentery!*

[The lights come up. The woman is seated on a chair
at center stage. Her hands strangle
one another in her lap.]

[A man in a lab coat strides in from stage left.
He appears to expostulate, holding out a white enamel
chamber pot.]

[The woman turns her face away. The lights go down.]

[Medical Officers' chorus]
> *She's a source of notoriety,*
> *and damaging publicity.*
> *Lock her up and lock her up for good.*
>
> *She is lacking all propriety.*
> *She's a menace to society.*
> *Lock her up and lock her up for good.*

[The lights come up. The woman stares out
a window frame, hanging at stage right.
In the distance, a cityscape, smudged by river mist.]

[A man enters from stage left. He takes a pencil
from behind one ear, and a notepad
from his pocket. He appears to expostulate.]

[She makes no move.]

[The man extracts a newspaper from inside his jacket
and tips it, as if it were a gentleman's hat, in her direction.]

[The lights go down.]

[Newspaper chorus]
> *Mary is rosy of cheek and buxom of form.*
> *A Walking Human Typhoid Germ!*

[The lights go up. The stage

is blank. The stage is

blank.

The stage is blank.

The lights go down.]

Mary Hardy Reeser

b. 1884? – d. 2 July 1951

CINDER LADY

1. *Dramaturgy*

A spectral bird above the mother's grave
(in Grimm); a pious godmother with magic
touch (Perrault). Fate must be *au courant*.
Her mask may be tragic

or absurd: Her lipstick is fashion's shade.
Fate steps onstage (a rooming house), her disguise
a sigh of barbiturate, a cigarette,
and Bette Davis eyes.

2. *Once upon a time, St. Petersburg, Florida*

Four *Seconal* and a cigarette will
do for Mary Reeser. Her acetate
nightgown is conjured to a jeweled gown
of flame. She levitates

from heavy dross to smoke. Her landlady
breaks in to a scene of soot and cinder
and one foot put primly forward, to be
fitted with its slipper.

Mari Sandoz

b. 11 May 1896 – d. 10 March 1966

AGAINST THE REDACTION OF MEMORY

1.

On the desk is an iron leaf, wrought
by a blacksmith who learned his trade
from Pancho Villa's gunsmith.

2.

Papa Sandoz had a soul of flint;
Its sparks gave light but little warmth.

Mari was snow-blind
in one eye, from tending his cattle
through a blizzard.

From his stories she made
a little bonfire of a book.

3.

Thousands of pottery sherds lie
upon a midden in Chaco Canyon.
On their convex surfaces, the patterns —
black-on-white, red-on-black —
are recurring and diagnostic.

On the fragments' reverse, unseen
when the pots were whole, marks left

by the potters' finger ridges —
indecipherable as the cliffs'
calligraphies of lichen.

4.

Among the pictographs at Cedar Mesa
are handprints, some of them
child-sized. Did a mother, bereft,
ever lean her cheek on the ochre
ghost of a dead son's hand,
and sing for him a last lullaby?

5.

He Dog, now an old man who was once
an Oglala warrior riding with Crazy Horse,
calls Sandoz *granddaughter*. Thunder rattles
its sabers while they talk, and he teases her:
You must come back in the dry season
and bring the rain again. But by then
He Dog is dead.

6.

(*Sandoz* page 408) Crazy Horse said to his murderers,
"Let me go, my friends. You have got me hurt
enough."

And later, dying, he whispered to his father,
(*Sandoz* page 413) "Tell the people it is no use
to depend on me anymore now."

Some deaths do not diminish over time.

Marianne Moore

b. 15 November 1887 – d. 5 February 1972

ARS POETICA: FOR MARIANNE MOORE

A Louis Comfort Tiffany
window, "secular,"
Hibiscus and Parrots. Among stark
blooms, two Carolina parakeets, raucous-
hued; one feeding, the other
yet in flight; circa 1910 to
1920 — concurrent with the species'
extirpation.
An illustration,
inadvertent, that creation
"with its capacity for
fact" possesses equally
capacity for loss. Contrary

as an extinct bird immortal
in glass, the Galápagos iguana is
machined from basalt, scale-model
locomotives scrap-
heaped on petrified lava flows, or,
Vulcan's mechanical cattle,
chugging
into the sea to rasp up algae.

The young Darwin tossed
one into a tidepool, again and again:
back it lumbered to its home rock

at his feet, undis-
suadable as iron to a magnet. It
shared "our own passional in-
ertia
against change, against
the effort of reason and the ad-
venture of beauty."

In repartee with Dame
Nature (her mordant
wit, every instance of it
fatal) you (exacting
ghost) devised your sprúng
poems, than which, *no
swan so fine.*

LEDGER

Does the air we vanish into taste of us, then?
SECOND DUINO ELEGY, Rainer Maria Rilke

1.

Suppose each star were named.
Suppose as each burnt down to cinders
someone mourned.
Suppose each scrap of paper
swirling through the streets
sang like a bird, suppose it spoke
the final words that fell
across its surface. Suppose
smoke had a memory.
Suppose it had a voice.
Suppose someone was listening,
someone with a pen and ink
and paper. Suppose there was
a list and that the clouds
could read it. Suppose they
broadcast it into space. Names
of stars. Names of birds. Names
called and no one answers.

2.

Ghosts of strangers rush out of this world
like doors slamming, and suck our hearts' blood
into that void. But it soon ebbs back. We cannot

sustain it, this tenderness for the unmet and
newly dead. Our mourning for them
is an ephemera. And so they languish

in some anteroom of grief, unattended.
They mill about, sip thin, terrible,
bitter coffee. And then set their cups

in saucers with a little *clink*, and turn
and go, seeing that we are faithless, no
use to them at all. Tatters of sorrow

blow after them. They do not turn to look.

3.
And if the day is dreary and smudged,
who will claim it?
If the hour is out at the elbows
and down in its heels,
who will stand up and take it home?
This tarnished minute,
this rusted week burning oil in blue smoke —
will anyone bid for it?
Time when nothing happens,
tedious time,
time with a headache
or an argument
or an unpaid bill past due
or the seconds just now passed —
who would miss them?
Ai Ai Ai
cry the voiceless dead reaching out
with their no hands.

Mary Makukutsi
b. ? – d. December 2007

REQUIEM for SISTER MARY MAKUKUTSI

INTROIT

On the plain by the Luangwa River

        we saw a whirlwind —

so vivacious, we thought it a dervish

    of swarming butterflies. It was leaves up-

showering in the fount of air.

  The whirlwind let fall the leaves

      and swept up a cloak of ash where

grass had lately burned. Dropped

    the ashes and turned to naked

  ghost shaking one mopané tree

        while all the rest kept still.

How swiftly, swiftly the soul discards

      the flesh by which we knew her.

KYRIE

Yambo we Lutanda —
    Hail, oh star —
We ulangé nshila ku benda mu mfifi —
    You who show the way to those who walk in darkness —
Uli ntungulushi!
    You are our guide!
Yambo we Lutanda —
    Hail, oh star —
Uletulombela fwe bamasambi —
    Intercede for us, who are sinners —
No mbaliné no mwaka wa kufwa kwesu.
    Now, and at the moment of our dying.

LECTIO PRIMA
Sarah visited by the angels (Genesis 18:1 – 15)

This morning's dawn was blood on the sky's hem.
Little swirls of wind lifted from the warming plain,
bearing dew's sweet smell and tickling the lambs
who leapt straight into the air with childish bleats.
The date palms sang with hidden birds.

Though no one noticed their coming, three men
stood in the palm shade by our tent. But they
were not men. I looked at them and knew they were
not men. Abraham knew it, too, and though I laid

my hand on his arm, he went to them and begged
them pause with us, and roasted them a calf
and had me bake them bread. They sat and ate

but tasted nothing, they drank but did not feel
cool water in their throats. Abraham spoke to them
and they replied but never heard his voice.
They are spirits, for all their sandals seemed
to stir the dust as they rose from seeming to eat.

They move within a radiance, guided by God's will.
And when the one turned his blind eyes on me
I laughed inside myself at what he seemed
to say. The angel knew I laughed, it was conveyed
to him that I had laughed. He chided me
and I felt afraid. So I will have a child

at last, a god-child who will gaze
on heaven, blind as these messengers
are blind — to sparrows bathing in dust, to blood
of women, to shawls of light thrown across the hills.
I am ravished by the Earth. I have been ravished
since I was a girl.

I will bear a child; I will love
him more than Earth; I will be driven to prayer
for his sake, and because he lives on after me
I will accept my exile into death. The sky
deepens into night. The stars are frost. The Earth
wraps herself in rich and scented shadow.
I shall not see her nakedness again.

DIES IRAE

Now we shall discuss in more detail the struggle for existence
by which this barren world evolved to be a garden of delights.
When earth has become a paradise, it will be a paradise of assassins.

A flower-spider unfurls her yellow legs among stamens,
and possesses herself in ambush. A leopard butterfly alights.
Now we shall observe in detail the struggle for existence,

whereby the living sustain themselves and undergo revisions.
Butterflies grow warier; spiders more cunningly disguised.
When earth reveals a paradise, it is a paradise whose assassins

are become exquisite. Under an acacia, a pride of lions
takes its ease. One lioness lifts her head — the green of her eyes
is the hiss of a struck match. It ignites a struggle for existence

among her prey. The sundew, turned on natural selection's
lathe, glistens with counterfeit honey. Milk and honeyed lies
have made the earth a paradise, and paradise, an assassin.

The forbidden fruit exhales its luscious fragrance; the mamba slides,
a rope of emeralds. Eve thinks of her handsome naked boy, and sighs.
God says: Now we shall discuss, in detail, your struggle for existence.
When I make Earth a paradise again, it will be a paradise of assassins.

OFFERTORIUM

What shall we offer as ransom, Lord,
      for the safety of her soul?
We who are ourselves forfeit,
      who ransom our lives with our lives?

The moon crouches down
      to lap dark water.
The stars shift, restless
      in their kraals.
With mortal eyes we see them.

The rain taps his drum,
      the drumhead stretched
to the rim of the world.
      The river fingers his kalimba.
With mortal ears we listen.

We who are ourselves forfeit,
      who owe our deaths for life's bounty —
What shall we offer as ransom, Lord,
      for the safety of her soul?

SANCTUS

Holy. Holy. Holy.
    Lord, your words breathe out fragrance of roses.
In crimson letters they herald the dawn,
    And at nightfall, conduct the sun to its rest.

Holy. Holy. Holy.
    Lord, your grace breathes out fragrance of roses.
She was showered with its petals at her birth.
    May she rest now in the bower of your grace.

AGNUS DEI

Luchelé Nyambi, Lucheyelé Lesa —
    Messenger of Light, Envoy of God —
Ne nkalamo aleshilopola, amalwelé aletundapa.
    Who hurls down the lions, and heals our ailments.
Luchelé Nyambi, Lucheyelé Lesa —
    Messenger of Light, Envoy of God —
Abana besu alebapa ubumi alebapa ifilyo.
    Who gives life to our children and nurtures them with food.
Luchelé Nganga —
    Healer and Envoy of Light —
Umwiné mutamba calo.
    You watch every corner of the world.

LUX AETERNA

Lolesha ubukata mulwelelé ukubeka kwanta pamo mo mweshi naka suba.

Look at the reign of heaven, the brilliance of stars and the moon.

The Southern Cross rises into glory of the Milky Way,

and shall rise, though one by one and kind after kind

we go into extinction. Behold: Among miombo,

termite mounds rise like half-formed animals

striving to quicken out of the Earth. For the clay

of Earth is ever fertile and shall not fail of life.

The Southern Cross rises into glory, and shall rise.

ABSOLUTION

We muteshina wakwa kampamba —
    Oh you, her guardian spirit —
Shikukula kuli Lesa Mukulu —
    Intercede to the Almighty God —
Ubwa lelo liné, twapapata.
    This very day, we beseech you.

IN PARADISUM

Towards dusk   thousands of

                   red-billed queleas come

flocking out of the veld

        to roost

             in thorn trees   smoke

    with wings   ashes with

                  wings

     what

       is Judgment Day but

   the Dead

     in their   scattered

parts

      rising thus

         a torrent   a surf-beat

   roiled molecules   the air   riven

             and pungent

      as from lightning

    flagrant scarves

       or a Colossus

         conjured   of weightlessness

                what is

     a symphony

       but beaked notes

pouring from staves   they   pause

        into the thickets

     spool aloft

          settle

            feather branches

      with clamoring foliage

   a fountain's droplets

splurging   up and   out   a galaxy
                                        both particle
and wave   what   is a species but this
                                        statistical cloud   ten-
dered
        to time and chance?

                    Darkness folds them
                    into the trees.

                Thousands of
                silences

                    fall.

                AMEN

                AMEN

                AMEN

Endnotes

THE LOST GOSPEL OF MARIA AEGYPTICA

Maria Aegyptica (St. Mary of Egypt) appears in various stories as a desert hermit of approximately the 5th century AD. In the most detailed version, she tells her history to St. Zosimas of Palestine, who encounters her (naked save for her unkempt hair) after she has lived in the desert for forty-seven years. She relates how she left her home at twelve, and lived in Alexandria for seventeen years, acting upon "an insatiable and irresistible lust."

She joined a pilgrimage to Jerusalem (though for no holy purpose), and when, curious, she attempted to enter the Church of the Holy Sepulchre, she was prevented repeatedly by an unseen force. Led by this event to repent her life, she crossed into the desert beyond the Jordan River, living in utter solitude there until meeting Zosimas, not long before her death. As the two converse, Zosimas observes several miraculous events: the woman levitates while praying, walks on the water to cross the river, and is clairvoyant.

MARIYAH THE COPT

Mariyah the Copt was a concubine of the Prophet Muhammad. Their son Ibrahim died in childhood, as did Muhammad's other two sons, by his first wife, Khadijah.

WHAT SHE KNEW

Marie Colinet's birth and death dates are unknown. She was already an experienced midwife when she married surgeon Wilhelm Fabry (Fabricius von Hilden), on 25 July 1587, in Geneva. She continued to gain skill and renown as a surgeon (she was made an honorary citizen of Paris in recognition of her work), and is known to have performed forty successful caesarean sections. She cared for Fabry's patients when he was absent, and continued to carry out surgeries on her own. In 1624 (as recorded in Fabry's *Centuriae*), she devised the method of using a magnet to extract a metal fragment from a patient's eye. She and Fabry had eight children, only one of whom outlived her. Wilhelm Fabry died in 1634; nothing is known of Colinet's life after that date.

Went and told them that had been with Him as they mourned and wept ... Mark 16:10
*Then arose Peter, and ran unto the sepulcher; and stooping down, he beheld the linen
cloths laid by themselves ...* Luke 24:12

MOLL CUTPURSE SINGS THE BLUES

Mary Frith was known in her lifetime by the nickname Moll Cutpurse. She was
arrested and charged with theft several times, was occasionally jailed, and once
committed to Bethlem Asylum ("Bedlam") for insanity. She was infamous (and
sometimes arrested) for dressing in men's clothing, smoking tobacco, and playing
the lute on the street, likely to draw a crowd that would then be pick-pocketed by
accomplices.

In their play about Moll, *The Roaring Girl*, Thomas Middleton and Thomas Dekker
have her speaking in "thieves' cant," a lingo of the London underworld. The play
was written during Mary Frith's lifetime, and she performed on stage at the play's
conclusion at least once.

"*Enter Moll in a frieze jerkin and a black safeguard*": Stage direction for Moll's first
appearance in *The Roaring Girl*. The costume is ambiguous: A jerkin is a man's jacket;
a safeguard is an outer petticoat, worn by a woman to protect her skirts from dirt.

The following canting words can be found in Nathan Bailey's *Canting Dictionary*,
published in 1736, and Francis Grose's *Dictionary of the Vulgar Tongue*, published in 1811.

Bing:	come or go
Partridges:	to "spring the partridges" was to lure in a crowd to be pick-pocketed
Cutpurse:	to pick-pocket, but also to castrate
Roarer:	one who drinks and brawls at taverns
Cloyer:	thief
Crew:	fellow thieves
Game:	persons drawn in to be robbed
Rigged:	clothed, outfitted
Stallion:	a whore-master, pimp
Lightmans:	daytime
Darkmans:	night

MARY EASTY

Mary Easty and seven other women and men were the last of those hanged who had been convicted of witchcraft during the witch trials in Salem Village. The trials began in March 1692. Bridget Bishop was the first to be hanged, on June 10. The trials and executions continued through the summer and early fall of that year. The others executed were Sarah Good, Rebecca Nurse (Easty's sister), Susannah Martin, Elizabeth Howe, Sarah Wildes, George Burroughs, John Proctor, John Willard, George Jacobs, Martha Carrier, Martha Corey, Alice Parker, Ann Pudeator, Margaret Scott, Wilmot Redd, Samuel Wardwell, Mary Parker, and Giles Corey. Five others died in jail: Sarah Osborne, Roger Toothaker, Ann Foster, Lydia Dustin, and an infant of Sarah Good. The bodies of the executed, being convicted witches, were not buried, but thrown onto the rocky slope below the hanging tree.

MARIA SIBYLLA MERIAN

Maria Sibylla Merian was the granddaughter, daughter, and stepdaughter of engravers and book publishers, in Frankfurt. She learned her crafts — painting and engraving — in their shops, and published several books in her lifetime, eventually supporting herself and her children, in Amsterdam. A correspondent (James Petiver) called her "That Curious Person Madame Maria Sybilla Merian," for she was an oddity in her time: divorced, a businesswoman and published artist, who traveled to Surinam, accompanied only by her youngest daughter, to study insects there. She also stood apart in her refutation of spontaneous generation through understanding of insect metamorphosis and ecology; her paintings were unique in depicting insects with their food plants, and in all stages of their life cycles. The poem's opening line was written by 18th-century entomologist René-Antoine Ferchault de Réaumur. I owe many details in this poem to Kim Todd's biography of Merian (*Chrysalis: Maria Sibylla Merian and the Secrets of Metamorphosis*).

When her husband was appointed ambassador to Turkey, Lady Mary traveled with him to Constantinople, where she learned to speak Turkish, and became well versed on the life, arts, and religion of the country, especially as they pertained to women. Her letters, written to family and friends, including Alexander Pope, were eventually published, as were many of her essays and poems, written before and after her time in Turkey. On her return, she brought with her the practice of "engrafting" (inoculation) against smallpox, which was widely practiced in Turkey, and which Lady Mary persuaded many (including England's royal court) to undertake.

The story of tortoises lighting the garden is told of Ahmed III, sultan during Lady Mary's time in Constantinople. See *Imperial Istanbul: A Traveller's Guide*, by Jane Taylor, Macmillan Publishers, Ltd., 1998, pp. 137-138. This was a sight Lady Mary did not see, as the Sultan's entertainments were for men only. The rest of the poem's details are from her letters. *Hammam* are the public baths of Turkey; the word *harem* is also Turkish, from the Arabic *harīm*, "forbidden place." Readers familiar with the formalities of the ghazal may care to know that my childhood nickname was "Minna."

THE WITCH

Maria Gaetana Agnesi was the first-born child of Pietro Agnesi, a wealthy merchant of Milan. She spoke seven languages, and at age nine composed a speech (in Latin) on the right of women to be educated. For a number of years, she devoted herself to the study of differential and integral calculus, found a solution to the curve that bears her name, and published a thorough introduction to the mathematics of Euler. She was the second woman appointed to a professorship at a university (the chair of mathematics and natural philosophy, Bologna). In later life, she directed the Hospice Trivulzio, working on behalf of the poor and the sick. She eventually joined the hospice's Order of the Immaculate Conception (the Blue Nuns). The "Great Hunger" in the poem refers to a famine of the 14th century. The last judicial executions for witchcraft/satanism were of two women burned at the stake in Poland in 1793.

"Prisoner number 280" was how Marie Antoinette was addressed during her final imprisonment. During her reign as queen, it was the fashion for wealthy women to wear elaborately decorated hats that celebrated current events: *à la circonstance*, *à l'Iphigenie*, and *à l'inoculation* were names of all such "topical" hats. She was convicted of various crimes by the Revolutionary Tribunal, and executed on 16 October 1793.

CHILDBED FEVER

Mary Wollstonecraft wrote *A Vindication of the Rights of Woman*, published in 1792. She detested the legal institution of marriage for its associated laws which made women into "gentle domestic brutes." At the same time, she asserted that women had strong sexual desires, and intellects to match those of men. All these views earned her condemnation. She eventually became the lover of an American trader, Gilbert Imlay, with whom she bore a daughter, Fanny. Imlay later deserted both Mary and their daughter. Mary's friendship with British intellectual and writer William Godwin grew into intimacy, and when Mary became pregnant, they decided to marry, in spite of their mutual misgivings about the institution. Shortly after giving birth to their daughter (also Mary, future author of *Frankenstein*), Mary Wollstonecraft died of childbed fever.

SHE GOES UPON THE STAGE AS ROSALIND

Mary Robinson (née Darby) became famous for her beauty and for her performances at Drury Lane Theatre, particularly in "cross-dressed" roles such as Shakespeare's Rosalind and Viola. She was mistress for a time to the Prince of Wales, who promised her an annual income in recompense for giving up her profession on the stage — and later reneged. Later in her life, after suffering an illness that left her partially paralyzed, she became known again; this time as a writer of poetry, novels, and essays (including several in defense of the rights of women, such as *A Letter to the Women of England, on the Injustice of Mental Subordination*).

"Men have died from time to time, and worms have eaten them, but not for love" is Rosalind's reply, in her guise as a young man, to Orlando, when he professes that love will be the death of him (*As You Like It*, Act IV, scene i).

SALT, A SLAVE NARRATIVE

Mary Prince was born into slavery in Bermuda. She was sent by her owner to Grand Turk Island, around 1802, to be a salt-raker there. Salt ponds were shallow pools, sometimes lined with clay, into which seawater was pumped, for the commercial production of salt by evaporation. The increasingly salty brine in the pools was called "bittern." The salt slurry was heaped into mounds for further concentration; the liquid which drained off was the "mother liquor." Prince's autobiography was among the earliest published firsthand accounts of the life of a slave.

STRATIGRAPHY

Mary Anning's father was both a carpenter and a collector and seller of fossils, in the coastal British town of Lyme Regis. He passed his fossil-hunting skills to his children before his early death, and Mary went on to become a well-known "fossilist," who unearthed a number of spectacular finds from the cliffs near her home. She once found a fossilized cuttlefish with its ink sac still intact; the painter Elizabeth Philpot used the ink to draw an image of the fossil. She sold the more common specimens to tourists (and was probably the subject of the tongue twister, "She sells seashells by the seashore"); the rarer ones — the first complete ichthyosaur in Great Britain, as well as the first known plesiosaurus, a pterodactyl, and others — were purchased for museums. The paleontologist William Buckland described her plesiosaur (which Georges Cuvier at first thought a fake) as looking like "a turtle with a serpent pulled through it." She wrote, "I do so enjoy an opposition among the bigwigs," in a letter in 1828. In spite of being a woman from a poor family, she became a self-taught expert in the anatomy and taxonomy of extinct species, and corresponded with the well-known scientists of her day. Visitors in her final years found her mental state confused at times; the cause was likely laudanum; she was dying of metastatic breast cancer.

Mary Ann Lamb was a writer, sister to essayist Charles Lamb, and friend to a number of their well-known contemporaries, including Samuel Coleridge. When Mary Lamb was 32 years old, she suffered a violent mental breakdown, during which she stabbed her mother to death and wounded her father. After a period of confinement in an asylum, Mary was released to her brother's care. For the rest of their lives, Mary and Charles lived and worked together. In 1807, they collaborated on a book for children, *Tales from Shakespeare*, that remains in print. (It is agreed that Mary was the primary author.) Mary continued to suffer episodes of severe mental illness (though without the violence of her first breakdown) during which she spent weeks or months in asylums. Between these periods, she was described by her friends as witty, keen of mind, and deeply kindhearted. In letters to their mutual friends, Charles occasionally wrote of what was otherwise unspeakable: their mother's coldness to Mary; Mary's horror at having killed her; and her unrelieved regret that she had, by that act, foreclosed all hope of the mutual affection she had longed for. The title is a line from a poem by Wallace Stevens.

COVERT ACTS

Mary Galloway was one among an unknown number of women who disguised themselves as men and fought in the American Civil War. She was seriously wounded in the Battle of Antietam, and when brought to the field hospital, her secret was discovered by Clara Barton.

Mary Edwards Walker was the first woman surgeon to serve in the United States Army. She was also an outspoken advocate for women's rights and welfare, including the right to wear unconstrictive clothing, and she was controversial for habitually wearing men's attire.

Mary Elizabeth Bowser was born a slave, manumitted on the death of her owner by his daughter (Elizabeth Van Lew), and sent then to the Quaker School for Negroes, in Philadelphia. Bowser and Van Lew conspired together to get Bowser employed in Jefferson Davis's "Confederate White House," in the guise of an illiterate slave, "Ellen Bond." Bowser regularly conveyed information from Davis's papers to U. S. Grant, via another spy, a baker making deliveries to the household. Bowser fled in 1865 when, at long last, she was suspected of being other than a dull-minded servant. Her last act on fleeing was an attempt to burn the Davis home. εἶδος: eidos.

ST. LOUIS CEMETERY NO. 1

Marie Laveau was a "free woman of color" who lived in New Orleans, and became famous as a "voodoo queen," though little is known with certainty of her life or practices. Her reputed crypt (where her daughter, at least, and possible successor as "Queen Marie," is interred) is visited by thousands yearly, seeking her favors and intervention. Traditions for doing so include circling the crypt three times, scratching three Xs on the crypt wall, and leaving various offerings. *Gris-gris*: a Caribbean or African amulet-charm. *Goofer dust*: a hexing powder, sometimes used as a synonym for graveyard dirt. *Yellow jack*: yellow fever. *Lwa* (also spelled "loa"): In Haitian vodou and Lousiana voodoo, spirit intermediaries between humans and Bondye, the "Supreme Creator."

MARY KELLY

Mary Jane Kelly was the last known and most savagely mutilated victim of Jack the Ripper. She was the only one of his victims whose death certificate gives the appellation "prostitute."

POSTHUMOUS LETTERS OF MARY HENRIETTA KINGSLEY

Mary Kingsley spent most of her first 30 years caring for her bedridden mother, while her father traveled the world as personal physician to wealthy clients, sending home vivid letters (frequently) and money (seldom). After the death of both parents in the space of a few weeks, Mary made her first voyage to the west of Africa. On subsequent journeys, she collected fish, insect specimens, and ethnographic information for the British Museum. She explored the interior of West Africa on foot and by river, with small parties of native guides, and all her personal equipage in a satchel slung over her shoulder. She taught herself the local languages, made her way by trading goods, and wore, without fail, full Victorian garb, including stays and full-length skirts. She became adept at handling both native canoes and the small European ships that plied along the coast. In 1900, she volunteered as a nurse for the wounded of the Second Boer War, and died of typhoid fever in a barracks hospital, in Simonstown, South Africa. She was buried at sea off the African coast.

The epigram is from a letter written by Kingsley to a man with whom she was in love; his response was to ignore the letter. Details of the "four souls" are from Kingsley's *Travels in West Africa*, as is the story of the "violet ball." Laplace's reported retort to Napoleon: *Je n'ai pas besoin de cette hypothèse.*

STAGECOACH MARY

"Stagecoach Mary" Fields was born a slave, in Tennessee, around 1832. Following the end of the Civil War, Mary worked for a time on the paddlewheeler, *Robert E. Lee*. Later, she worked at an Ursuline convent in Toledo, Ohio, and eventually followed some of the Sisters who befriended her to Montana, where she was put in charge of construction of the mission. Mary stood over six feet tall, weighed over 200 pounds, and had no fear of a fight, whether with her fists or a gun. The bishop of the Montana diocese, finding this behavior unseemly, ordered her dismissed from the mission. In the years that followed, Mary ran a restaurant and laundry, and became the second woman to carry mail for the U.S. Postal Service (from the town of Cascade, to the Ursuline mission, nineteen miles away). She lived in Cascade until her death, an avid fan of the local baseball team, and favorite caregiver to the town's children — including the young Gary Cooper.

TESTIMONY

On March 25th, 1911, a fire broke out on the 8th floor of the Triangle Shirtwaist Company in New York City. The fire quickly spread to the floors above, fed by scraps of pattern paper and cotton fabric, piled in bins under the worktables. In less than twenty minutes, 146 workers (mostly women) were dead. Some burned to death inside the factory. Some jumped or fell down the elevator shaft. Many jumped from the windows and died on the sidewalks below. Others were crushed to death when the fire escape collapsed under their weight, shortly after Mary Bucelli fled by that route. Among the dead were Mary Goldstein (age 18, identified by buttons on her shoes), Mary Herman (age 40), Mary Leventhal (age 22), Maria Manara (age 27), and Mary Ullo (Gullo? Age 26?). The poem's first section is drawn entirely from testimony at the trial, later that year, of the factory owners. They were found not culpable for the deaths, though survivors testified that they found the exit doors locked, and the one fire escape nearly inaccessible. The identity of the woman who tossed her hat and coins from her pocketbook, before jumping to her death, is unknown; several witnesses in the street described her final actions.

GHOST BIRDS

The names and descriptions of Hawaiian birds are from *A Field Guide to the Birds of Hawaii and the Tropical Pacific*, H. Douglas Pratt, Phillip L. Bruner, and Delwyn G. Berrett (Hawaii Audubon Society, 1987). Native Hawaiian birds have suffered the greatest rate of extinction of any bird fauna. The women's names are from the 1920 federal census of the (then-named) Kalaupapa Leper Settlement on Molokai, Hawaii. Starting in 1866, and until isolation laws were repealed in 1969, about 8,500 people suffering from Hansen's Disease were taken from their families and communities, and confined to Kalaupapa until their deaths. They were referred to in the census as "inmates." The census also recorded whether each had attended school, was able to read or write, and whether she had a trade.

MARY CASSATT, AFTER 1915

Mary Cassatt became an artist despite the lifelong objections of her father. She left America for Paris to study her art, though women were not yet admitted to the École des Beaux-Arts. Eventually she was befriended by Degas, and associated for a time with the Impressionists. Later she was much influenced by Japanese prints, and made a series of brilliant drypoints and aquatints. She was known among her fellow artists as "The Independent" for her unblunted opinions and the determination with which she pursued her art. Though she is best known for her unsentimental but deeply felt portrayals of mothers and children, she decided early on that motherhood and a life in art could not coexist. She chose her work. Cassatt began to lose her sight around 1914, and by 1915 was no longer able to work in any medium.

RADIUM

Marie Curie was born Maria Salomea Skłodowska, in Warsaw, Poland, and emigrated to Paris to study physics and mathematics at the Sorbonne. She discovered the element radium in 1898, eventually isolating a few grams of it from ten tons of pitchblende. She was the first woman to win the Nobel Prize, for physics in 1903, and again in 1911 for chemistry.

The remark about ants' shadows was actually made by Devin James Pearl, then age six, while exploring after dark in Canyonlands National Park, in 2004.

From the *New York Times*, "As to Picturing the Soul," 24 July 1911: "Dr. Duncan MacDougall of Haverhill, who has experimented much in the observation of death, in an interview published here to-day expressed doubt that the experiments with X-rays about to be made at the University of Pennsylvania will be successful in picturing the human soul, because the X-ray is in reality a shadow picture. He admits, however, that at the moment of death the soul substance might become so agitated as to reduce the obstruction that the bone of the skull offers ordinarily to the Roentgen ray and might therefore be shown on the plate as a lighter spot on the dark shadow of the bone." MacDougall was famous for his efforts to find the mass of the human soul by weighing dying persons just before and after death. He found the soul to weigh less than an ounce.

"Heaven doth with us as we with torches do": *Measure for Measure*, Act I: Scene i.

Mary Mallon, an immigrant from Ireland who worked as a cook for a series of well-to-do families, was taken into custody in 1907 by the New York City Health Department, having been identified as the first-known "healthy carrier" of typhoid fever in the USA. She was confined to North Brother Island (then a hospital and isolation island, mostly for tuberculosis patients), where her feces were collected and tested, weekly, 163 times, until she was released in 1909. In 1915, she was discovered to be working under the name "Mrs. Brown" at Sloane Maternity Hospital, during an outbreak there of typhoid fever. She was returned to North Brother Island, where she remained until her death 23 years later. She never accepted the experts' findings that she was the source of typhoid infection in the hospital and seven households where she had worked. The "newspaper chorus" lines are taken from the *New York American* newspaper, April 2, 1907. New York children are said to have chanted the first line of the "children's chorus" while at play in the streets during the years when "Typhoid Mary" was infamous.

CINDER LADY

In October 1952, *Pageant Magazine* published an article by Dr. Wilton Marion Krogman, titled "The Strange Case of the Cinder Lady," about the death of Mary Hardy Reeser, whose body was found in her one-room apartment by her landlady. Reeser's left foot, in a sateen slipper, was unburned; the rest of her body was reduced to ash and charred bone (the chair in which she was sitting was also burned to cinders). Reeser's death has often been described as a case of spontaneous combustion, though forensic scientists (beginning with a study by the FBI at the time of the event) have concluded that she fell deeply asleep (having taken, according to her son who spoke to her the previous evening, four sedative tablets) and dropped her cigarette, which ignited her nightgown and afterwards her body and chair.

Mari Sandoz was born Mary Susette Sandoz, to Swiss immigrants, in the Sandhills of Nebraska. She was educated at home until she was nine, and did not speak English until she began attending school. She completed the eighth grade at age seventeen, and began teaching in rural schools to help support her family. Eventually she studied at the University of Nebraska, and worked as a proofreader and researcher for the Nebraska Historical Society. Her first published book, *Old Jules*, was a collection of stories from her father's hardscrabble pioneer life. Among her many other books was *Crazy Horse: The Strange Man of the Oglalas*. She traveled thousands of miles to visit places that figured in the life of Crazy Horse and to interview those still alive who had known him.

Frank Turley made for me the iron leaf of the first stanza. Turley worked for a time with Victor Vera, who was commandeered when in his teens by Pancho Villa to repair guns and break open safes.

ARS POETICA

Marianne Moore, American poet, critic, essayist.

"secular": From the Metropolitan Museum of Art's exhibit of Tiffany works: "The window's small size and secular subject suggest that it was intended for a domestic setting."

"with its capacity for fact": See Moore's poem, "An Octopus."

"I threw one several times as far as I could into a deep pool left by the retiring tide; but it invariably returned in a direct line to the spot where I stood": Charles Darwin, writing in *The Voyage of the Beagle* of his 1835 visit to the Galápagos Islands.

"our passional inertia…": Randolph S. Bourne's characterization of the response of the American people to the State's war-blandishments during the Great War, from his posthumously published (1919) essay, *The State*. Dos Passos wrote of Bourne:

> *If any man has a ghost,*
> *Bourne has a ghost, a tiny twisted unscared ghost*
> *in a black cloak hopping along the grimy old brick & brownstone streets still*
> *left in downtown New York …*

...which, minus "twisted" (Bourne was afflicted with severe scoliosis), describes Moore, Bourne's fellow and contemporary New Yorker, equally well.

"No swan so fine": See Moore's poem by that name.

LEDGER

September 11, 2001. Mary Jane (MJ) Booth, 64 • Mary Katherine Boffa, 45 Mary Ellen Tiesi, 38 • Mary D'Antonio, 55 • Mary D. Stanley, 53 • Mary Melendez, 44 Mary S. Jones, 72 • Mary Kathleen Shearer, 61 • Mary Lou Langley, 53 Mary (Molly) Herencia, 47 • Mary Lou Hague, 26 • Mary Rubina Sperando, 39 Maria Isabel Ramirez, 25 • Mary Trentini, 67 • Mary Yolanda Dowling, 46 Mary Jo Kimelman, 34 • Mary Lenz Wieman, 43 • Mary Teresa Caulfield, 58 Mary Wahlstrom, 78 • Rosa Maria (Rosemary) Chapa, 64 • Margaret Mary Conner, 57 Susan Mary Bochino, 36 • Joanne Mary Cregan, 32 • Rose Mary Riso, 55 Linda Mary Oliva, 44 • Eileen Mary Rice, 57 • Jean Marie Wallendorf, 23 Jeannine Marie Damiani-Jones, 28 • Marie Lukas, 32 • Jill Marie Campbell, 31 Manette Marie Beckles, 43 • Dolores Marie Costa, 53 • Lisa Marie Terry, 42 AnnMarie (Davi) Riccoboni, 58 • Marie Pappalardo, 53 • Katie Marie McCloskey, 25 Michelle Marie Henrique, 27 • Leanne Marie Whiteside, 31 • Jean Marie Collin, 42 Cira Marie Patti, 40 • Laura Marie Ragonese-Snik, 41 • Diane Marie Moore Parsons, 58 Anne Marie Sallerin Ferreira, 29 • Rosemarie C. Carlson, 40 • Alison Marie Wildman, 30 Donna Marie Giordano, 44 • Donna Marie Rothenberg, 53 • Maria Jakubiak, 41 Maria Percoco Vola, 37 • Maria Lavache, 60 • Diane Maria Urban, 50 Rosa Maria Feliciano, 30 • Maria Theresa Santillan, 27 • Maria Rose Abad, 49 Maria Behr, 41

REQUIEM FOR SISTER MARY MAKUKUTSI

Sister Mary Makukutsi was a Catholic nun, and nurse, whom I met when she worked at a health clinic in a rural district outside Lusaka, Zambia. She died of illness in 2007.

INTROIT: Mopané means "butterfly" in one of the native languages of Zambia. The leaves of mopané trees are shaped like butterflies.

KYRIE is Bemba (one of the native languages of Zambia), with each line followed by its English translation; the two are to be read as call and response. The lines are from a traditional hymn to Mary, and from the Bemba version of the "Hail Mary." These and the other Bemba prayers in the poem were found in *Bemba-Speaking Women of Zambia in a Century of Religious Change*, by Hugo F. Hinfelaar, published 1994. Hinfelaar points out the central role that veneration of Mary, Mother of Christ, played among Bemba-speaking women who were early converts to Catholicism.

The first refrain line in the *DIES IRAE* is from Charles Darwin's *On the Origin of Species*. The second refrain line is from Wallace Stevens's poem, "Life on a Battleship." Leopard butterflies and sundews are native to southern Africa, as are green mambas.

OFFERTORIUM: The kalimba is the traditional "thumb piano" of African music.

SANCTUS: Christian monks of Ethiopia still prepare illuminated manuscripts of sacred texts, in which the words spoken by God are written with a red ink prepared from rose petals. Many of those served by the clinic where I met Sister Mary are families of workers at a nearby rose farm.

Before contact with Christianity, there was already, among Bemba-speaking people of Zambia, a tradition regarding the coming of a "healer" or "messenger of light" who would arrive from the East. Some of the lines of the *AGNUS DEI* are adapted from a praise song written for an early Catholic bishop in Zambia (Hinfelaar).

LUX AETERNA: Miombo is a type of open woodland typical of Zambia, named for the most common tree species of the habitat. In a traditional creation story of Zambia, God uses the clay of termite mounds to make all Earth's animals.

ABSOLUTION is from a traditional prayer said on behalf of a child suffering from illness (Hinfelaar).

IN PARADISUM: Red-billed queleas are drab birds, about the size of sparrows. They are one of the world's most numerous bird species, and their roosting flocks can number in the tens or hundreds of thousands.

Biographies

MELINDA MUELLER

Melinda Mueller trained as a biologist and is on the science faculty at Seattle Academy of Arts & Sciences. Entre Ríos Books published her most recent book, *The After*, as a collaboration with Karinna Gomez and the Syrinx Effect. Her book *What the Ice Gets: Shackleton's Antarctic Expedition, 1914 – 1916* (Van West & Company, 2000) received a 2001 Washington State Book Award and the American Library Notable Books Award for Poetry in 2002. Her other books of poetry are *Private Gallery* (Seal Press, 1976), *Asleep in Another Country* (Jawbone Press, 1979), and *Apocrypha* (Grey Spider Press, 1988). Melinda was a coauthor of an early list of rare, threatened, and endangered plant species of Washington State.

LORI GOLDSTON

Classically trained and rigorously de-trained, possessor of a restless, semi-feral spirit, Lori Goldston is a cellist, composer, improvisor, producer, writer, and teacher from Seattle. Her voice as a cellist, amplified or acoustic, is full, textured, committed, and original. Best known for her work with Nirvana, Earth, and the Black Cat Orchestra, she is a relentless inquirer and wanders recklessly across borders that separate genre, discipline, time, and geography, performing in clubs, cafés, galleries, arenas, concert halls, sheds, ceremonies, barbecues, and stadiums. You can listen to and learn more about Lori's work at her site, www.lorigoldston.com.

About the Art

The publisher wishes to express gratitude to artist Karen LaMonte for her generous use of images for this book. Exploring the body in absentia and how identity and society intersect with women's coverings, she has worked in a variety of mediums, and is best known for her life size sculptures of disembodied women's clothing in glass, bronze, and ceramics. The cover image, *Reclining Dress Impression with Drapery*, is cast glass and is found in the permanent collection of the Smithsonian American Art Museum and the Renwick Gallery Collection.

The end papers, *Incidence (Dress)*, are earlier explorations of this theme, using large presses to make life-size prints of dresses, which LaMonte calls Sartoriotypes.

Her work is avidly collected and found in the permanent collections of museums, worldwide. To learn more about her art and her process, please visit her website at www.karenlamonte.com.

Audio

To download a recording of Melinda Mueller reading from this book, as well as the music by Lori Goldston, please visit our website, www.entreriosbooks.com/audio. Select this title and enter the password:

THOUSAND BELLS

Melinda Mueller recorded at Skoor Sound, Seattle, Washington
Recorded by Naomi Siegel and Eric Eagle
March 25, 2017

Lori Goldston: *Cello Songs for Mary's Dust*
This suite of five songs was commissioned specifically for this book.

1. The Dust of a Thousand Bells
2. Mariyah the Copt
3. Love's Bitter Stings / Love's Bitter Strings
4. Her Daughter
5. Offertorium (Matthew)

Recorded live at the Chapel Performance Space, Seattle, Washington
Recorded and mastered by Mell Dettmer
February 23, 2017

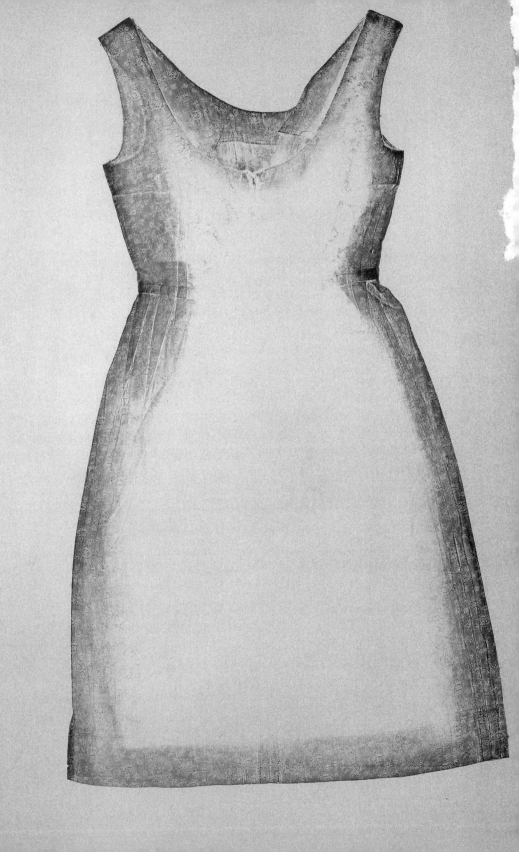